40 DAYS OF REFLECTION

Devotions for Lent

THOMAS A MAYBERRY

Thomas A Mayberry

40 DAYS OF REFLECTION

First Printing, 2022

This book is dedicated to my mom and dad. They laid the ground work for my life. Bringing me up in a Christian environment and nurturing my faith in my early years led me to pursue a deeper relationship with God later in life. I am deeply indebted to them for teaching me the core values that I needed. I can only hope I can be as good of an example to others as they have been in my life.

Contents

I

Prepare your Heart

"I have been crucified with Christ and I no longer live, but Christ lives in me. The life I now live in the body, I live by faith in the Son of God, who loved me and gave himself for me."

Ash Wednesday marks the first day of the 40 days of Lent, a six-week period (excluding Sundays) dedicated to prayer, fasting and reflection in preparation for celebrating Christ's life, death and resurrection. It is the beginning of a season which calls us into self-analysis, deeper reflection about God's grace and mercy, and a sense of generosity towards those most in need.

The ancient practice of Ash Wednesday reminds us that we are mortal. It causes us to pause, look at our lives, and remember what we are made of and where we are going. It encourages us to fully immerse ourselves in the Lenten season.

...For you were made from dust, and to dust you will return.
Genesis 3:19 (NLT)

Death and resurrection are not a one-time thing as our life on earth ends and our eternal life in Heaven begins. Each time we let go of the past and embrace the future, we start a new life. Each time we allow our fears, pride, bitterness.....we start a new life. We need to open ourselves to the Spirit so that we can break down the walls that separate us from God. What do you envision as the new life you are aiming for?

Prepare your heart today for that new life. Pray for God's forgiveness regarding the areas of your life that are standing in the way of a close relationship with Him. Give up the temptation to have full control over your life and your future. Remember, it is not your will that you should be striving for, but God's will that you should be fulfilling.

That is why the Lord says, "Turn to me now, while there is time. Give me your hearts. Come with fasting, weeping, and mourning. Don't tear your clothing in your grief, but tear your hearts instead." Return to the Lord your God, for he is merciful and compassionate, slow to get angry and filled with unfailing love. He is eager to relent and not punish.
Joel 2:12-13 (NLT)

God doesn't want an outward display of repentance without true inward repentance. We should not repent just with our words; we need to give Him our whole heart! He knows what we are thinking and how sincere we are. He wants us to come back to Him even as we have strayed away. God is patient and merciful; He loves us so much that He welcomes us back.

I have been in the food service business my whole career and have prepared many meals from recipes. Preparing something is the act of putting something together, to make ready beforehand for some purpose, use or activity. The result we are looking for in this instance is a closer relationship with God. Prepare your heart so that you can come back to God and start a new life in Christ's image. Let Him guide your ways. If we listen to Him, we He will give us the recipe we need to prepare our hearts.

I pray that this season of Lent brings you closer to God and helps you celebrate Christ's life, death, and resurrection.

2

Forgiveness – Pay it Forward

Yesterday, we reflected on our sins and letting them die so that we can have a new life with Christ. We have repented and through Jesus dying on the cross, we are forgiven. Addressing our sins and asking for forgiveness is only one step that God wants us to do. We must also forgive those who have hurt us. We pray that in the Lord's prayer, but do we do a good job of it? Most of us do not.

"Pray then like this: Our Father who art in heaven, Hallowed be thy name. Thy kingdom come, Thy will be done, on earth as it is in heaven. Give us this day our daily bread; and forgive us our debts, as we also have forgiven our debtors; and lead us not into temptation, but deliver us from evil."
Matthew 6:9-13 (ESV)

When we do not forgive each other, we carry that burden with us. The other person probably has moved on and is no longer affected by what they did. We continue to harbor anger, frustration, stress, sadness and a wide array of other feelings. When we can forgive someone, we can let that action and the associated feelings die and start a new life.

"Get rid of all bitterness, rage and anger, brawling and slander, along with

every form of malice. Be kind to one another, tenderhearted, forgiving one another, as God in Christ forgave you."
Ephesians 4:31-32 (NLT)

Why is it that we have such a hard time forgiving someone? Is it because we want justice? We want them to suffer for what they have done. Maybe we want karma to pay a visit. We carry some anger with us because it does not feel fair that they are forgiven because if we forgive them, it is like we condone their behavior. Forgiving others may seem to be a choice, and in one sense it is a choice, but God has been very clear about forgiveness. He has given us specific direction in numerous Scriptures, all of which can be summed up in just one word -- forgive!

And when you stand praying, if you hold anything against anyone, forgive them, so that your Father in heaven may forgive you your sins."
Mark 11:25 (NIV)

Who has hurt you that you have not forgiven? How is it affecting you? What feelings do you have for that person because of it? Do you have bitterness, anger, resentment, or possibly a desire for revenge? These toxic emotions do not change the situation or the person that hurt you. They are only hurting you. In Colossians 3:13, it says *Make allowance for each other's faults, and forgive anyone who offends you. Remember, the Lord forgave you, so you must forgive others.* This is part of the Lord's prayer that we ask for. We ask for forgiveness as we have forgiven others. This means we need to hold up our end of the bargain. We must forgive others.

Here are a couple of ways to help you in the forgiving process. Practice stress reduction techniques. Keeping a cool head helps you stay calm and rid yourself of the toxic emotions. Sometimes the person you need to forgive is a family member. Remember why it is important for them to be in your life. Let that feeling guide your decisions.

Pray that God will give you the strength to forgive the person who has hurt you and allow you to move forward with your life.

3

Train up a Child

How are our children going to follow God's direction? Can they understand when God is speaking to them...telling them where He wants them to go and how He wants them to act? It is our responsibility as parents to be sure our children see Christ in us.

Proverbs 22:6 says, *"Direct your children onto the right path, and when they are older, they will not leave it."*

We must set an example for our children in all aspects of our lives. Pray for them and teach them how to pray. Develop in them habits of worship, service, encouragement, forgiveness and honesty. There are many traits of God that our children need to learn. Dependability, integrity, trust, cooperation/teamwork, kindness, and honesty are a few.

When I was young, my mom taught me a lesson about honesty that has stuck with me to this day. As a young boy growing up in a small town, I went to the grocery store to buy some penny candy with 25¢ that my mom had given me. As I was leaving, I went to the soda machine and hit the buttons to see if a drink would fall out...and it did! I was so happy. Not only did I have a bag of candy, I also had a nice cold drink to sip on during the bike ride home.

When I got home, my mom asked where I got the soda knowing how much money she had given me. When I explained how I got it, she told me I would have to go back to the store and pay the cashier for the drink. Even though someone else *had* paid for the drink, I had not. With that logic, mom gave me a quarter and I went back to the store to pay for my drink.

Are you teaching your children about honesty, and many other similar traits, in such a way that these traits stick with them for a lifetime? How we talk and behave around our children will mold them as future adults. I pray I have been a positive role model, and have adequately taught Christ's traits, to my two sons. We start our children on their walk with God so that when they get older, they will be more aware of God's will and direction in their life.

As Christian parents, we have an obligation to teach values to our children so they will know how to respond to and treat others. On the other hand, this does not need to be an overly complicated process. It comes down to two main principles that the Bible teaches us.

Love God. The first part of Luke 10:27 says, *He answered, "Love the Lord your God with all your heart and with all your soul and with all your strength and with all your mind"*. He wants us to love Him with our whole being. By doing that, we can see situations and other people from His point of view.

Love others. The second part of Luke 10:27 says, *"... and, "Love your neighbor as yourself."* We care if someone steals from us, and we care if someone lies to us. Therefore, we should act with honesty and integrity toward others because we don't like it when others treat us in the wrong manner.

Emphasize to your children the importance of knowing God— knowing Who He is, His character traits, and how He wants every one of us to know Him and personally walk with Him.

4

Walk on Water

Immediately Jesus made the disciples get into the boat and go on ahead of him to the other side, while he dismissed the crowd. After he had dismissed them, he went up on a mountainside by himself to pray. Later that night, he was there alone, and the boat was already a considerable distance from land, buffeted by the waves because the wind was against it. Shortly before dawn Jesus went out to them, walking on the lake. When the disciples saw him walking on the lake, they were terrified. "It's a ghost," they said, and cried out in fear. But Jesus immediately said to them: "Take courage! It is I. Don't be afraid." "Lord, if it's you," Peter replied, "tell me to come to you on the water." "Come," he said. Then Peter got down out of the boat, walked on the water and came toward Jesus. But when he saw the wind, he was afraid and, beginning to sink, cried out, "Lord, save me!" Immediately Jesus reached out his hand and caught him. "You of little faith," he said, "why did you doubt?"
Matthew 14:22-33 (NIV)

Do we trust in God's will even if it means we go into unknown territories where we may feel uncomfortable? Do we trust in Him only when things are going our way? I have experienced tough times in my life and have wondered "why me?". At the time I thought God should have spared me some of the agony since I was His faithful follower.

Giving God full control of our lives is not an easy task. People tend to want to be in control. We like to know where we are going and be able to make decisions about which way to turn along the way. However, if we want to follow God's will, we need to trust in His judgement and His plans for our future.

Jesus told His followers to anticipate problems. We should not be surprised when we go through a tough season in our lives. God knows it is coming, he warned us about it, but will be with us **all the way.** He will help us overcome everything that comes into our lives.

"I have told you all this so that you may have peace in me. Here on earth you will have many trials and sorrows. But take heart, because I have overcome the world." John 16:33 (NLT)

We live in an instant gratification world. We are very impatient and with modern technology, we have become even more impatient. We need to learn to be patient for God's will to play out.

My thoughts control my mood and attitude. I'm guessing that's true for you, too. We need to keep our focus on God and not the worldly issues going on around us. It's important to remember that even when we forget God, He never forgets us! He knows what's happening to us every moment of the day, and He also watches over us. The reason is because He loves us with a love that never fades.

He asks us to pray continuously. You can have conversations with Him throughout the day. Whether it is over a cup of coffee before going to work, or during your morning commute. It may be nonverbal, just a thought that crosses your mind. It does not need to be in the formal way that we think about prayer and conversing with God.

Test your faith. Take the steps needed to give more control of your life over to God. You will be amazed at the results. Because He has such an imagination for your future, you will experience things you never dreamed of on your own!

5

Prepare for the Journey

Do you have a trip planned for your vacation later this year? What do you do to prepare? Perhaps you put together a task list that may include the following. Make airline and hotel reservations. Check out local attractions and what days and hours they are open. Make a list of clothes and personal belongings to take. We do a lot of planning to make sure that everything goes just right.

As Jesus was walking beside the Sea of Galilee, he saw two brothers, Simon called Peter and his brother Andrew. They were casting a net into the lake, for they were fishermen. "Come, follow me," Jesus said, "and I will send you out to fish for people." At once they left their nets and followed him. Going on from there, he saw two other brothers, James son of Zebedee and his brother John. They were in a boat with their father Zebedee, preparing their nets. Jesus called them, and immediately they left the boat and their father and followed him.
    Matthew 4:18-22 (NIV)

This Scripture tells quite the opposite story compared to how we prepare for a trip. Can you imagine dropping what you're doing and following someone without knowing where you're going or what you'll be doing? That concept is so foreign to us. We want to be prepared. Peter and his brother did not tell Jesus "We need to go home first and get our belongings together. We will meet up with you in a little while." They immediately left their nets and followed Him. James and John left their father, and their boat, to follow Jesus. I wonder what their father thought at the time. Perhaps Zebedee thought his sons were taking a great leap of faith! Today, we can see who Jesus is through studying the Bible. The disciples, however, were experiencing Jesus firsthand at the early part of His ministry.

Too often, we want to be completely prepared and wait for just the right moment to do things. That causes us to potentially miss out on opportunities that God puts in front of us. We need to learn how to trust God in our direction in life. You do not always need to know the outcome of trying something new or wonder if you have everything that you need to be successful. God has already done all the planning and makes sure that you have everything that you need.

For I know the plans I have for you, declares the Lord, plans for welfare and not for evil, to give you a future and a hope.
   Jeremiah 29:11 (NIV)

Sometimes we go through tough times. When we are facing difficult situations today, we can take comfort in this verse knowing that it is not a promise to immediately rescue us from hardship or suffering, but rather a promise that God has a plan for our lives and regardless of our current situation, He can work through it to prosper us and give us a hope and a future. But what if everything is going our way and we think we are in control? Do we trust His direction? What are you willing to give up, or walk away from, to follow Jesus? Have you felt called to do something by God? How did you approach it? Did you hesitate for a bit before buying into God's plan or did your faith allow you to trust in the outcome Prepare your heart to accept God's direction in your life and trust His plans.

6

Turn to Scripture

Faith in God, and His direction for our life, is sometimes confusing. Most of us have probably asked God, at some point, for a sign. After decades of trying to write a book and not coming up with the words, I prayed one night in 2010, "God, give me a sign to show me if I should continue trying to write a book or if I should forget about it and move on to something else."

In the middle of the night, I woke up with the phrase "Faith Based Leadership" on my mind and understood that the approach to my book on leadership needed a change. I realized the main reason I was so passionate about sharing the traits of a good leader was not due so much to my work skills but was guided almost entirely by my faith in God. I changed my direction, and my first book was published within nine months.

Not all direction comes from experiences like the one I had that night. We do, however, have a place to go to get the direction we need. If you read the Scriptures, it will speak to you and give you the answers you are seeking. You need to remember, though, it may not always give you the answer that you want to hear. It is God's will we need to follow and not our own.

All Scripture is inspired by God and is useful to teach us what is true and to make us realize what is wrong in our lives. It straightens us out and teaches us to do what is right. It is God's way of us in every way, fully equipped for every good thing God wants us to do.
2 Timothy 3:16-17 (NLV)

I admit I do not have a regular, set routine for reading my Bible. Some people do it when they first wake up or with their morning cup of coffee. Others have a devotional book they follow every day. I guess you can say that I binge read. Do not consider yourself a bad Christian if you do not have regular Bible study. Whatever works for you is acceptable in God's eyes. He has provided this resource to speak to us and loves when we listen to Him.

I am always amazed when I read a Bible verse or hear a sermon that is exactly what I needed to read or hear at that moment in time. I know God is watching over me and guiding me through the day. Look to the Scriptures to see what God wants you to do and where He wants you to go. What a blessing it is to know we have a Father who will guide us through life never leaving our side. Thank you, Lord!

This verse resonates with me. It goes back to trusting God's plan in my life. It guides me to know what my responsibility is in the plan.

"Commit to the lord whatever you do, and he will establish your plans."
Proverbs 16:3 (NIV)

If you act in the way He wants you to act, He will produce the plan in front of you. Are you treating others the way you want to be treated? Are you putting God's approach first and foremost in your everyday behavior? We do not always have that fork in the road where we need to decide as to which way to turn. If we are instep with God, it will be clear where He wants us to go and what to do next.

7

Living by the Holy Spirit

We worship a triune God...the Father, the Son and the Holy Spirit. We speak easily of God the Father and of Jesus Christ, His Son, but we generally do not put as much emphasis on the Holy Spirit. Galatians 5:19-26 reveals how our lives are enriched when we are open to the Holy Spirit's guidance. We also learn of the hardship suffered when we are closed to the Holy Spirit.

"When you follow the desires of your sinful nature, the results are very clear: sexual immorality, impurity, lustful pleasures, idolatry, sorcery, hostility, quarreling, jealousy, outbursts of anger, selfish ambition, dissension, division, envy, drunkenness, wild parties, and other sins like these. Let me tell you again, as I have before, that anyone living that sort of life will not inherit the Kingdom of God.

But the Holy Spirit produces this kind of fruit in our lives: love, joy, peace, patience, kindness, goodness, faithfulness, gentleness, and self-control. There is no law against these things!

Those who belong to Christ Jesus have nailed the passions and desires of their sinful nature to his cross and crucified them there. Since we are living by the

Spirit, let us follow the Spirit's leading in every part of our lives. Let us not become conceited, or provoke one another, or be jealous of one another."

We all have sinful inclinations that we need to deal with. Some of them are obvious like sexual immorality, lust, idolatry, and drunkenness. Others we tend to overlook and let them into our lives like hostility, jealousy, anger, and selfishness. Verse 24 says that we need to crucify them. Let them die so that we may be born again. If we follow the desires of a sinful nature, we will not inherit the Kingdom of God. That is powerful! But that is not all. We worship a just God who is also merciful.

If we willingly nail our sinful nature to the cross and accept Jesus Christ as our Savior, we are forgiven. By doing this, it allows the Holy Spirit to work within us. With the Holy Spirit working within us, we can experience love, joy, peace, patience, kindness, goodness, faithfulness, gentleness and self-control. These are referred to as the fruit of the Spirit. When we choose the direction of the Holy Spirit, we would inherit the Kingdom of God.

I think if I took a poll, it would be unanimous that option #2 is the better choice. What can you do to increase the fruit of the Spirit in your life? What can you do to separate yourself from the items in the first scenario? Focus on the Holy Spirit working within you.

When a believer is led by the Holy Spirit, they will obey God's Word, and go in the direction that He wants them to go. God speaks to us in our hearts and shows us the way we are to go. When you don't know what to do in each situation, you can ask the Holy Spirit and He will give you the solution.

Many times, we want to know the will of God for our lives and one way we can is by listening to His Spirit. It is such a blessing to receive the gift of the Holy Spirit.

Allow the Holy Spirit to come into your life and guide you along the way. It is a triune God that we follow, and the Father, Son and Holy Spirit *all* play a role in our lives.

8

Using your Gifts

All of us have talents and these talents are a gift from God. They make us unique and uniquely able to complement one another. If we all had the same talents, though, life would be dull and boring. Everyone's talents and personalities blend to get things accomplished and make the world a beautiful place.

Imagine an orchestra in which everyone played the same instrument. It would not be as beautiful and diverse as an orchestra with many different instruments being played. In a similar way, when God created us, he gave each of us different instruments to play. Among God's children there are introverts and extroverts, creative people and analytical people, leaders and followers, those who love to cook and those who don't. The list of talents and characteristics that make us unique is endless.

Peter, in his first letter, tells us to be a good steward of our gifts and to use them to glorify God as we serve others.

Just as each one has received a gift, use it to serve one another as good stewards of the varied grace of God. Whoever speaks, let it be with God's words. Whoever serves, do so with the strength that God supplies, so that in everything

God will be glorified through Jesus Christ. To him belong the glory and the power forever and ever. Amen.

1 Peter 4:10-11 (NET)

On a recent move I was deciding the part of town in which to live. I wanted to find a church where I could use my talents to serve others. Once I found a church, I then looked for a nearby house to purchase. My pastor presented a vision of starting a community food pantry which would bring together many of the area churches to provide food for the less fortunate. I knew right away I wanted to be a part of this effort. I felt a calling from God.

Starting up the food pantry was not an easy task. We needed a wide variety of talents, as well as the willingness to use those talents, for God's glory. Volunteers were needed to serve on the board of directors as well as in a variety of hands-on jobs required to collect, stock and distribute pantry items. After months of planning and preparation by many people with many different talents, the doors were opened to serve those in need.

How are you serving others? How are you using your gift? Have you considered being a mentor? Are you a handyman that can perform small repairs? Perhaps you can drive an elderly neighbor to a doctor's appointment. Serving can be as simple as giving joy to others.

As we serve, God will show us what our gifts are, and he will reveal his calling for us. How can you serve others at work, at school, at home, and in your community?

9

God Smiles on Us

To whom do you look for advice? Is it a parent, a friend, a co-worker? Perhaps you rely on digital media for advice or information. That may be OK in some instances, but for the important issues in life, we need to seek God's advice and direction. Keep your eyes and focus on God. He will speak to us through Scripture, through other Christians, and through the Holy Spirit inside of us.

The steps of the godly are directed by the Lord. He delights in every detail of their lives. Though they stumble, they will not fall, for the Lord holds them by the hand. Psalm 37:23-24 (NLT)

We honor God when we trust in Him and strive to do His will. This pleases Him and He watches over our every step. When we follow His will, He gives us a firm footing so that we do not fall, however, when we lose our focus on Him, we will surely stumble.

Have you ever tripped because you were not paying attention to the ground in front of you? Our relationship with God is very much like that. Early in my career, I pushed hard to climb the corporate ladder as I sought a more powerful and higher paying position. I lost track of the importance of my family, my marriage and regular church attendance.

Quite frankly, when looking back, I'd become distracted by worldly things and had slipped away from God.

Throughout this time, God never left my side even though I was not paying attention to Him. He was there to hold my hand and, when I acknowledged His presence, He helped me to re-balance my life. He is faithful to His followers. There is a saying that goes "God is smiling down on me." When we are following His will, He delights in pleasing us. He loves to see us happy and praising Him for what He has done. He can do so much in our lives if we let Him. If we pursue His will, and not our own, He blesses us with things that we cannot even imagine.

One of the most powerful reminders to me of the greatness of God is the starry night sky. He created all the stars in the sky. The size of it all is beyond our imagination. Scientists tell us that our galaxy is 100,000 light years across. One light year is 5.76 trillion miles. There are billions of galaxies in the known universe. Some astrophysicists theorize there may even be universes beyond our own. It is hard to visualize wat we cannot see.

Too often, we limit what we think God can accomplish in our lives by what we can imagine. He can do so much more. He can do anything and everything. We need to learn how to let go of our plans and let God direct us. Let Him create paths we cannot even imagine. By doing this, we allow Him to bless us beyond our reality.

Let us all pray that we can focus on God and trust, with faith, that His will is best for us. We can rely on the paths to which He directs us because He has already taken care of all the details.

10

What is around the corner?

Do you know what is around the curve in the trail? When living in Nashville, I was regularly on a greenway, so I knew what to expect around each curve. Our life, though, is not as easy to predict. God sometimes changes our paths, just as He did with Joshua. After Moses died, the Lord spoke to Joshua, Moses' assistant. God wanted him to lead His people across the Jordan river to the land that He was giving them. This is what God told Joshua:

I command you—be strong and courageous! Do not be afraid or discouraged. For the Lord your God is with you wherever you go.
Joshua 1:9 (NLT)

Some people are afraid to try something new because they do not like change. They stick with jobs that are unsatisfying just because they fear what will happen if they change companies. But sometimes God changes career paths for us! In doing so, He may open opportunities we never even knew existed or put us into a position that fits our skill set perfectly. In such a circumstance, we will probably enter a period of uncertainty, however this is where our faith in God should kick in and comfort our minds. He may provide opportunities we were not even looking for as He navigates our course with us.

God will always provide for our needs even if it means we must go through some lean years financially. Such times allow us to appreciate that what is important is not money and things, but family, relationships and being a blessing to others. For example, I have a friend who would take food to the homeless only to have them ask if it was OK to give most of it away to their friends. Wow! Even in their time of need, they were thinking of others!

I can reason that if God is leading me to do something, then it should be a smooth ride. Unfortunately, that's not always so. Leaving something that you love because God has called you to something new takes courage. I'm learning that courage must be developed like a muscle, and this doesn't happen on its own. God expects me to do my part, and that involves not only taking the first scary step but also trusting Him with each step after that.

I travel a lot for work and am told, regardless of what state I am in, "If you don't like the weather, just wait a little bit". It will change. Everything changes. Ecclesiastes 3 tells us that life is full of seasons and seasons are always changing. This is not something that we can avoid.

This is good news because it reminds us that if you don't like your current circumstances, you can rest assured that they will inevitably change. When change comes and the transition from one season to the next can feel shaky and the details unclear. When life is uncertain, and things are up in the air, we must remember and cling to the fact that God is steady.

We don't know what lies ahead, but all our experiences should be viewed as learning opportunities. Go around that unknown curve in your path. You may find that the view is better on the other side. Remember that your journey of life is a long path; it is a scenic trail with numerous bends, dips and hills.

Now, get out there and enjoy your greenway!

11

Constant Communication

God calls us to live our life in constant communication with Him. How is that possible? When I'm in any place with loud background noises, I have a hard time concentrating on, and hearing, what others are saying. With our busy lives, we may also have a hard time hearing what God is saying. We, therefore, need to adapt to our circumstances.

Look for times to converse with God throughout your cluttered day. Talk to Him about your activities. Tell Him about your joys, your sadness, your confusion and needs. Remember, your goal is not to fix things or to take control away from God. It is to acknowledge your dependence on Him and to communicate with Him.

Rejoice always, pray continually, give thanks in all circumstances; for this is God's will for you in Christ Jesus.
1 Thessalonians 5:16-18 (NIV)

When we think of prayer, we think of a quiet time when we block out our surroundings and tell Him our needs and praises. I used to be confused when reading this verse, not knowing how I could pray all the time. I now realize it means having a prayerful attitude in all we do, acknowledging God's presence, and speaking with Him throughout the day whether in spoken words or silent thoughts.

When you see something beautiful in nature, thank God for it. If you experience great joy, thank Him for the opportunity. When things are not going as planned, ask for His guidance to get you through the situation. There are limitless times throughout the day we can communicate with God.

Seek Him in all you do, and he will direct your paths.
  Proverbs 3:6 (NLT)

Just as you rely upon the GPS system in your car, so you don't make a wrong turn, rely also upon God to be your spiritual road map guiding you throughout your day. If you maintain sight and communication with God, He will direct your path and keep you from going the wrong way.

I do not want to skip over the first part of 1 Thessalonians 5:16 which says to rejoice always and give thanks in all circumstances. That seems awfully tough when you're having a bad day, a bad week or a tough year. When you look back on your life, you can look back on those tough times and realize that God used them to prepare you for something greater. Therefore, be thankful for God's presence during the rough stretches and for what he accomplished in you during the hard times. He has great plans for you...and for all his children!

Celebrate God in everything you do, stay in constant communication with Him and He will lead you where you need to go.

12

As for Me

Do know someone who has a plaque on their wall that reads *"But as for me and my household, we will serve the Lord"*? This comes from the time Joshua told his people they needed to make up their minds. Honor and worship the Lord our God...or worship the gods and idols that their ancestors worshiped. They could not have it both ways.

But if serving the LORD seems undesirable to you, then choose for yourselves this day whom you will serve, whether the gods your ancestors served beyond the Euphrates, or the gods of the Amorites, in whose land you are living. But as for me and my household, we will serve the LORD." Then the people answered, "Far be it from us to forsake the LORD to serve other gods! It was the LORD our God himself who brought us and our parents up out of Egypt, from that land of slavery, and performed those great signs before our eyes. He protected us on our entire journey and among all the nations through which we traveled. And the LORD drove out before us all the nations, including the Amorites, who lived in the land. We too will serve the LORD, because he is our God." Joshua said to the people, "You are not able to serve the LORD. He is a holy God; he is a jealous God. He will not forgive your rebellion and your sins. If you forsake the LORD and serve foreign gods, he will turn and bring disaster on you and make an end of you, after he has been good to you."

But the people said to Joshua, "No! We will serve the LORD." Then Joshua said, "You are witnesses against yourselves that you have chosen to serve the LORD." "Yes, we are witnesses," they replied.

Joshua 24:15-23 (NIV)

We must make that choice every day. Do we trust in God and put Him first in our lives, or do we have other priorities? Are we obsessed with money and objects? Do we adapt to the ways of the world if it is easier? When we put these things as a priority before God, we are worshiping them. Joshua took a stand and said that it did not matter what the others decided to do. His mind was made up.

I have had situations in my life where co-workers had priorities that did not align with what I thought God wanted for me. I had to decide if I would alter my beliefs to conform to those around me or if I was going to take a stand. I was not always accepted due to my beliefs, but I held firm. God stayed with me through it all and I am reaping the rewards He has given me for my loyalty to Him.

Joshua's people spoke all the right words by saying they would serve the Lord and obey only Him. It is easy to say the words, but did their (or our) actions follow their (or our) words? In the case of the Israelite's, which we can read about in Judges, they once again slipped away from the covenant they made with the Lord that day.

Lord God, help us to keep our covenant with you. Give us strength to turn away from the idols of the world and to keep our focus on you. Regardless of what others may do, as for me and my household, we will serve the Lord!

13

A way out

Our Father who art in heaven, hallowed be thy name. Thy kingdom come.
Thy will be done on earth as it is in heaven. Give us this day our daily bread,
and forgive us our trespasses, as we forgive those who trespass against us, and
lead us not into temptation, but deliver us from evil. For thine is the kingdom
and the power, and the glory, forever and ever. Amen.

Christians pray the Lord's prayer more often than any other prayer.
There are different versions based on denomination, but it is the same
prayer with the same meaning. With the pressures of today's society,
and the behaviors seen all around us, it is easy to ignore or forget the
lessons of the past.

The Bible is filled with examples of the Israelites going against God's
will. In Paul's letter to the Corinthians, for example, he told them
about the consequence suffered by some of Moses' followers who chose
to worship idols, feast and drink heavily and even engage in sexual
immorality. As a result, 23,000 died in one day. You do not want to
experience the wrath of God! Paul had warned the Corinthians to stay
true to their covenant with God and follow His direction. The same
warning is given to us through Scripture.

So, if you think you are standing firm, be careful that you don't fall! No temptation has overtaken you except what is common to mankind. And God is faithful; he will not let you be tempted beyond what you can bear. But when you are tempted, he will also provide a way out so that you can endure it.
  1 Corinthians 10:12-13 (NIV)

Isn't that amazing! Because our God also has a loving, merciful side, He has given us a way out! When we pray "lead us not into temptation", we're asking God to keep us from *giving in* to the temptation. But God has promised, through His faithfulness to us, that He will not let us be tempted beyond what we can bear. This sparks the question, "How much can I bear?" Satan will tempt all of us, but it seems as though he targets Christians the most. Do you suppose Satan takes pride in stealing someone away from God?

As the phrase from The Art of War goes, "Know your enemy." Knowing the enemy is a crucial aspect of any battle. As Christians, we have many enemies, one of which is our own nature that lingers within us. It may seem odd, but we must study ourselves. Personality, circumstances, temperament, and experiences are all factors that can make us more susceptible to certain kinds of temptations. How can we be on guard for something unless we know what we are up against?

We can, however, resist the temptation Satan puts before us. We can utilize the *way-out* God has so lovingly provided. I am reminded of a time when my son was a senior in high school and chose to spend the 4th of July with us. his family, instead of his friends. When asked why he was not going out with friends, he explained there would be drinking going on and he chose not to be around it. He told his friends he had plans with his family. That makes a parent proud! God provided a way out for my son. When you are tempted, He will provide a way out for you, as well!

14

Time to Listen

We gain wisdom when we listen more and talk less. Too often, we are thinking about what we will say next instead of listening to the person speaking to us. We do not give them our full attention. How much do we listen to what God is saying? In Jesus' time, people had to really listen to what He said and remember it to be able to gain knowledge. They did not have the opportunity to see it in print and re-read it whenever they want.

We can now have the Bible on an app on our phone. We have access to it all the time. I sometimes think our modern technology has made it so easy to hear the Word that we hardly hear it at all. Our lives are so complicated we do not pay as much attention to anything.

My dear brothers and sisters, take note of this: Everyone should be quick to listen, slow to speak and slow to become angry, because human anger does not produce the righteousness that God desires.
James 1:19-20 NIV

We need to make it a priority to improve our listening skills. Verse 19 also tells us to be slow to speak. There is a time to speak and a time to be silent. Most of us are better at the former and not so good at the latter.

Proverbs 29:20 talks about it this way. *There is more hope for a fool than for someone who speaks without thinking.* When we do most of the talking in a conversation, it comes across like we feel our ideas are more important than the other person's. We need to slow down, listen to what other people have to say and then decide how to answer. It is too easy to have our minds made up about a response before the person has finished.

The Harvard Business Review explains that there are three elements of "active listening".

Cognitive: Paying attention to all the information, both explicit and implicit, that you are receiving from the other person, comprehending, and integrating that information

Emotional: Staying calm and compassionate during the conversation, including managing any emotional reactions (annoyance, boredom) you might experience

Behavioral: Conveying interest and comprehension verbally and nonverbally

To be good at the cognitive aspect, you must really be paying attention and observing besides listening. Our reactions (behavior) can really show how much we are listening. One of the hardest aspects is to keep our emotions in check. That is especially important in an argument.

When you quit listening to what the other person is saying and just argue your point, it is easy to get angry. The angrier we get, the faster we speak, and the less we hear. We can avoid a lot of the anger in an argument if we would listen to what the other person is saying....... truly hearing what they are saying. Lord, help us take time to listen.

15

Good Samaritans

"By chance a priest came along. But when he saw the man lying there, he crossed to the other side of the road and passed him by. A Temple assistant walked over and looked at him lying there, but he also passed by on the other side. "Then a despised Samaritan came along, and when he saw the man, he felt compassion for him.

Luke 10:31-33 (NLT)

What thoughts do you have when you read this parable? Does it upset you that people would just pass by and not help someone in need? Do you say to yourself "I would stop"? How many times do we pass by a person in need because "someone else" can help them?

Have you seen cell phone video of a terrible event and wondered why someone was filming instead of stepping in to help? Have you personally witnessed someone being harassed but you did not intervene? We've all been in a situation when someone is talking badly about another person. Do we step in and defend the person? If not, do we choose to ignore the situation or possibly even join in on the negative talk? Why is that? Why don't we get involved? Is it that we are too busy or feel it's not our problem?

In other cases, we see people who risk their life to pull someone from a burning car or house. They don't think twice about jumping in to help. What makes them different than the people in the previous scenarios? Jesus' parable talked about the religious men who passed by a person in need but ignored him, while the despised Samaritan was the one who stopped to help. That hits home! We, as followers of Christ, are taught from His teachings how to love one another. This is a blessing we should not take lightly.

Jesus came into this world to rescue us. He gave His life for us. That is so powerful! In response to His love and sacrifice, we are given the opportunity to love our neighbors and jump in when needed.

There are opportunities all around us. Co-workers who are harassed, talked about behind their backs, down on their luck, suffering emotionally. We should not just pass by someone who is stranded on the side of the road with no one to help. We assume they have a phone and can call for assistance. People who have lost their homes to natural disasters such as tornadoes and hurricanes. They need enormous amounts of help. What will we do in circumstances such as these?

Sometimes the need is not something physical or materialistic. Sometimes it is emotional. Are you preparing a holiday meal and are aware of someone who is going to be by themselves for the holiday? Have you considered inviting them to your house? I have done this on occasion, and it was a blessing to both them and me.

We all want to be a better neighbor. We all want to love our neighbor as ourselves. It's the getting started that's so darn hard, isn't it? We can always find a reason for passing by, but now is the time for everyone to step up and be good Samaritans to those around us who are in need.

16

A Fresh Start

Have you ever wanted a fresh start on your career path, in your relationships, or for mistakes you've made? Consider the story of the woman Jesus met at the well in Samaria.

Soon a Samaritan woman came to draw water, and Jesus said to her, "Please give me a drink." The woman was surprised, for Jews refuse to have anything to do with Samaritans. She said to Jesus, "You are a Jew, and I am a Samaritan woman. Why are you asking me for a drink?" Jesus replied, "If you only knew the gift God has for you and who you are speaking to, you would ask me, and I would give you living water."
John 4:7, 9-10 (NLT)

Twice each day, morning, and evening, most of the Samaritan women drew water from the well. But the woman in our story did not get water at the normal time with everyone else. Because of her reputation, this woman went during the middle of the day in order to go unnoticed. It was during her solo trip to the well that she encountered Jesus.

When she saw Him, she prepared herself for the worst because He was clearly a Jew, and she knew full well the Jews were prejudiced against Samaritans. John 4:18 also tells us the woman had been married several times in the past and was currently living with another man. While it is clear Jesus knew the woman's reputation, He nevertheless valued her and spoke to her with respect.

The good news Jesus shared with the Samaritan woman is for everyone regardless of race, social status or past sins. He offered her the living water of the Holy Spirit, who lives among us and guides our path. With the acceptance of Jesus Christ as our Savior and the guidance of the Holy Spirit we will have eternal life. In doing this, Jesus gave the Samaritan woman a fresh start.

You may be at a point in your life where all you can see is a mess—regrets, wrong turns, shame or broken relationships. Are you embarrassed and wish there was a restart button? Jesus sees past your mess and can give you a fresh start. He wants to set you free from your burdens. He offers you living water so your thirsty soul will be satisfied. But what does Jesus mean when He's talking about living water? He gives us the answer in John 7:38-39:

Anyone who believes in me may come and drink! For the Scriptures declare, 'Rivers of living water will flow from his heart.' (When he said "living water," he was speaking of the Spirit, who would be given to everyone believing in him. But the Spirit had not yet been given, because Jesus had not yet entered into his glory.)
John 7:38-39 (NLT)

With the Holy Spirit comes eternal life. Let Him give the living water, the Holy Spirit, and eternal life to you. This will give you a fresh start. So, the first step of embracing your fresh start with God is by fully embracing the truth that no matter what has happened in your life, you are still righteous before God if you have placed your faith in Jesus Christ. Your righteousness is now based on Christ and not your own actions. It is time to take that first step towards a fresh start.

17

Better than a Pool

One man was there who had been an invalid for thirty-eight years. When Jesus saw him lying there and knew that he had already been there a long time, he said to him, "Do you want to be healed?" The sick man answered him, "Sir, I have no one to put me into the pool when the water is stirred up, and while I am going another steps down before me." Jesus said to him, "Get up, take up your bed, and walk." And at once the man was healed, and he took up his bed and walked. Jesus came to the pool of Bethesda, where there were crowds of sick people lying by the pool. Legend said an angel came down and stirred the pool's water once in a while. The people believed that the first person to get to the pool after that would be healed. And so everyone lay there, day after day, watching the water to see if it would move. One man had been there 38 years!

John 5:5-14 (ESV)

Jesus spoke to him: "Do you want to be healed?" On the surface, this sounds like a foolish question. Of course, the man wanted to be healed! Why else would He come to Bethesda? Perhaps the man thought it was a foolish question, too. Who knows? At any rate, the man didn't answer Jesus. Instead, he complained. He couldn't get into the pool fast enough -- someone else always got there first. That's why he could never get well. Or so he thought.

Jesus did not care about the excuses, for with Him, nothing is impossible. "Get up," He said. "Take up your bed and walk." Much to his surprise, the man did! He got up and found himself completely healed. The pool was unnecessary. Jesus healed him!

We are like that man, too, aren't we? When we fall into sickness or trouble, we seek the best help we can find. We turn to doctors, lawyers, social workers or experts -- anybody who can offer us hope in our situation. And we are right to do it because God has given these people talents for our protection and help.

But we are even wiser when we turn to Jesus and ask Him to help us. He is the giver of all good things; He is our Creator and our Redeemer. He cares so much for you; he willingly chose to suffer and die on the cross. Now, as our risen Lord, absolutely He will care for you now, in your need. We need to turn to Him, and He will provide for us, with or without other people's involvement.

God is the ultimate healer! Too often we think it is just sickness that we need healed from. Yes, He can heal us physically from our sickness, injury or disease. He also heals us from emotional pain. Sometimes emotional wounds can be deeper and more painful than physical injuries or illnesses. The absence of parental love, the pain of rejection or betrayal, the unexplainable sorrow of losing a child, spouse, or anyone you deeply loved, can all seem incurable. God never designed us to experience that kind of grief and sorrow.

Jesus heals those kinds of wounds that can't be cured through surgery, medication, or a positive attitude. Psalm 147:3 tells us *"He heals the brokenhearted and binds up their wounds."*

Do you have a problem loving someone? Forgiving someone? Moving on past a certain hurt because your mind keeps replaying it? What do you need healing from?

Lord Jesus, You know my sickness. Please help me however You see best. Amen.

18

A Want or a Need?

Christians can overcome the temptation of worldly desires by making a purposeful decision to be content. A believer can trust God to provide their true needs, and not be consumed with materialism. There is not a promise of wealth, or even an easy life. The concept of "need" must be considered according to God's will. What we "need" and what we "want" are not always the same thing. God tends to bless those who will use the resources they have according to His purposes.

And my God will meet all your needs according to his glorious riches in Christ Jesus.
Philippians 4:19 (NIV)

Most people **want** to avoid discomfort and pain in their lives. God may not provide everything we want but *will* take care of our needs. We need comfort and support when we go through trying times and He will be there for us. He gives us an example by comparing us to the birds and the fields.

Look at the birds of the air; they do not sow or reap or store away in barns, and yet your heavenly Father feeds them. Are you not much more valuable

than they? Can any one of you by worrying add a single hour to your life?
"And why do you worry about clothes? See how the flowers of the field grow.
They do not labor or spin. Yet I tell you that not even Solomon in all his
splendor was dressed like one of these. If that is how God clothes the grass of
the field, which is here today and tomorrow is thrown into the fire, will he not
much more clothe you—you of little faith?

Matthew 6:26-30 (NIV)

So many people worry about what may not go as they have planned. There is nothing wrong with thinking about what could go wrong so you have back up plans. Do not, though, stress about the possibilities of negative events. God *will* provide your needs. As it says in the previous Scripture, if He can take care of the needs of the birds and clothe the fields with flowers when they can't provide for themselves, He will take care of us.

I have been living stress free ever since writing *Stress Free Living, Is it possible or just a dream?* Part of the process of becoming stress free is to believe God will take care of my needs. I know I have many "wants" and those will not all become reality. If I truly trust God to provide for my needs, I will not feel the negative things that go on. I will not stress over the "what ifs".

Needs can be classified into two types: Food, clothing, water, oxygen and shelter are all physical needs. On the other hand, psychological needs are emotional kind of needs. These needs are; the need to belong, the need to pursue one's goals, the need for attachment, or the need for control. You may feel these are true needs, but can you survive without them? Yes. Think about what would happen if you did not have one or more of these needs.

If you really put things into perspective, the worst-case scenario is not as bad as you may think. Always ask yourself, is it a "want" or a "need" and them remember God will take care of your needs. It is all in the attitude.

19

Why Matthew?

Jesus chose twelve people, with different backgrounds, to be His disciples. Matthew, a tax collector, was one of the chosen few. When asked by Jesus to be His disciple, Matthew immediately followed Him. In the same way, Simon (Peter) and Andrew dropped their nets to immediately follow Jesus as well. It was different for Matthew, however. The others could go back to fishing, but Matthew could not go back to collecting taxes after he walked away from his tax booth. So why would Jesus pick Matthew?

As Jesus went on from there, he saw a man named Matthew sitting at the tax collector's booth. "Follow me," he told him, and Matthew got up and followed him. While Jesus was having dinner at Matthew's house, many tax collectors and sinners came and ate with him and his disciples. When the Pharisees saw this, they asked his disciples, "Why does your teacher eat with tax collectors and sinners?"

On hearing this, Jesus said, "It is not the healthy who need a doctor, but the sick. But go and learn what this means: 'I desire mercy, not sacrifice.' For I have not come to call the righteous, but sinners."

Matthew 9:9-13 (NIV)

Matthew was a tax collector. Even today, most people do not like having to pay taxes and it was not much different in Jesus' time. Tax collectors, including Matthew, were despised because they would collect more than what was owed and keep the extra for themselves. It was, in fact, a very lucrative career. In verse 13, Jesus explains He is not looking for the righteous, but for sinners...and Matthew fit the bill!

I grew up knowing this story, but I didn't realize there was another reason for picking Matthew. God has plans for all of us and He's given us talents to use to glorify Him. In Matthew's career as a tax collector, he needed to keep good records and pay attention to details. This made him an ideal candidate to follow Jesus, to observe and record what was going on around Him. The Gospel bearing his name records the greatest story ever told.

God gives us all skills and abilities with which to serve Him. Our past doesn't matter when we get His calling. We *will* be called to follow Him, to start a new life. If you have already been called, did you immediately drop what you were doing and follow Him? Did you wonder, "Why me?" Are you using your talents to serve Him, through others? If you have not been called yet, what will be your response when that time comes?

"Now there are varieties of gifts, but the same Spirit. And there are varieties of ministries, and the same Lord. There are varieties of effects, but the same God who works all things in all persons."

1 Corinthians 12:4-6 (NASB)

What talents has God given you? Today is a good day to take an honest inventory of all the abilities God has endowed you with. And more importantly, ask yourself: Why has God given me these talents? Better yet, ask God why.

Dear God, what one thing do You want me to do today, to use the talents You have given me?

20

The Cost of Following God

During Jesus' ministry, He used a lot of examples, some of which were hard to understand. Therefore, He told parables in order to illustrate the principles He was teaching. In the teaching about the cost of following Him, He used comparisons in nature.

As they were walking along the road, a man said to him, "I will follow you wherever you go." Jesus replied, "Foxes have dens and birds have nests, but the Son of Man has no place to lay his head." He said to another man, "Follow me." But he replied, "Lord, first let me go and bury my father." Jesus said to him, "Let the dead bury their own dead, but you go and proclaim the kingdom of God." Still another said, "I will follow you, Lord; but first let me go back and say goodbye to my family." Jesus replied, "No one who puts a hand to the plow and looks back is fit for service in the kingdom of God."
Luke 9:57-62 NIV

Jesus wanted the man to follow Him but there was no guarantee where it would lead. There was no promise of a "place to lay his head." When we are asked to follow God, there is not a plan showing where we are going or how we will get there. Luke does not tell us if the second man's father was terminally ill or already dead. It is thought if he were already dead, the man would have been home taking care of funeral arrangements instead of walking with Jesus. And while Jesus doesn't teach us to ignore family obligations, He knew the man's excuses indicated he was not ready to put Christ first in his life. True discipleship requires immediate action even if it requires a personal sacrifice.

God wants total dedication. We can't pick and choose which of Jesus' teachings we will follow based on what fits our current situation. We are not promised the easy life where we get all the good things but none of the struggles. Jesus died for us and our salvation. There are costs in following God. We may need to avoid things and people, even family members in some cases, in order to follow God's principles. Have you heard people say they put God first in their lives, even above their family? This is what it means to be fully committed to God.

When people are gambling in card games, like poker, there is a phrase of "I'm all in". It means they are betting **all** their chips (money) on the outcome of that hand. They are taking a major chance that they will have a favorable outcome. They have confidence that the odds are in their favor.

If we follow Jesus, the odds are in our favor that there will be a favorable outcome. This does not guarantee an immediate favorable outcome like winning a hand in poker. But we are risking what lies ahead. If we are satisfied with our life and the direction it is going, do we want to risk that to go down God's path for us? Are you ready to accept whatever cost may be involved to follow God?

Do fully committed followers of Jesus go to church a lot, give a lot of money, volunteer, pray a lot, etc.? Often, yes, but the activity itself isn't the relationship. The activity is merely the conduit, opening the capacity for God to show himself to us and lead us closer to his heart. Fully committed disciples discover, more and more each day, what it is to be spiritually free. To avoid anything that prevents them from a richer experience of God's presence.

21

Work Together for Good

In the same way, the Spirit helps us in our weakness. We do not know what we ought to pray for, but the Spirit himself intercedes for us through wordless groans. And he who searches our hearts knows the mind of the Spirit, because the Spirit intercedes for God's people in accordance with the will of God. And we know that in all things God works for the good of those who love him, who have been called according to his purpose.
Romans 8:26-28 (NIV)

Starting in early 2020, we were in the middle of a global pandemic with the coronavirus. We were directed to socially distance ourselves from others. Businesses closed their doors, people worked from home, and restaurants had to adjust the ways they serve their patrons. Thousands of people around the globe contracted this disease, which at times was fatal. It has put a lot of fear into people not knowing what the future has in store for them. Will they and their loved ones stay healthy—will they continue to have employment?

When the needs of the world are so overwhelming, we can be at a loss for words when we pray. We are weak and suffering and need widespread healing to save lives. We turn to you Lord in our helplessness. Thankfully, we are not praying alone; The Holy Spirit intercedes for us. As we do not know God's will in this situation, we need to ask the Holy Spirit to bring our requests to God in harmony with His will. His will may be for us to act instead of crying for help. Or we may even be the help that someone else is crying out for through their prayers.

We can serve those in need. It may mean food for the hungry or comfort for the scared. It may be shopping for the elderly, so they don't have to go out. God is working **through us** to bring goodness in trying times.

In fact, God works in "everything", not just isolated incidents, for our good. This does not mean that everything that happens to us is good, but He will turn every circumstance around for our long-term good. As our scripture for today says, those who love God have been called according to this purpose. God's goal is for us to be like Christ. We can accomplish this by accepting Christ as our Lord and Savior, reading and following the Word, spending time in prayer, being filled with the Holy Spirit and doing God's work.

Having faith in God is easy when life feels both comfortable and blissful. In these seasons we often feel as though God is nearby. Naturally, we interpret these good experiences as good. However, the times where life feels uncomfortable and problems abound, we feel disconnected from God.

English writer John Heywood coined "Two heads are better than one" in 1546. I am sure he did not realize he was speaking prophetically. But two heads together can work only when God is at the center. King Solomon wrote, *"Two people are better off than one, for they can help each other succeed. If one person falls, the other can reach out and help. But someone who falls alone is in real trouble"* Ecclesiastes 4:9-10

As things are getting better for us after the pandemic, let's not forget to work together for the good of others.

22

Do not Fear

We are currently living in uncertain times. We went through a pandemic, are on the edge of a recession, and there is a major war going on in other parts of the world that makes us worry if we are on the verge of a third world war. This brings with it fear and anxiety. We fear what could happen to ourselves and our loved ones. In the beginning, the fear was for our health but has now escalated to include the economy and its effect on us personally and globally. In a previous devotional, we learned about wants versus needs. Our fear and anxiety during these turbulent times should be lessened knowing God will take care of our needs but is it enough?

So do not fear, for I am with you; do not be dismayed, for I am your God. I will strengthen you and help you; I will uphold you with my righteous right hand. Isaiah 41:10 (NIV)

Yes, it is enough! God tells us He is always with us, and we can turn to Him for strength and help. In my experience, this is what it means to lean on God: believing in His Word, giving all my cares to Him, and trusting Him no matter what. I am thankful to have His grace, mercy, and strength to carry me through good times and bad.

I love this passage: *"Humble yourselves, therefore, under the mighty hand of God so that at the proper time He may exalt you, casting all your anxieties on Him, because he cares for you."* 1 Peter 5:6-7 ESV

It takes humility to realize we need help. It likewise takes humility to accept help...whether it comes from other people or even if it comes from God. We must trust God fully with our lives and recognize that He will always take care of us. Do not give in to fear regarding current circumstances over which you have no control. God still has power and authority over every circumstance!

To make that easier to understand, think about this: when you give something to someone else, it's now theirs to take care of; it no longer belongs to you nor is it your responsibility. The same thing happens when you give your fears and anxieties to God. They are no longer your concern. Don't let fear and anxiety about your health, the economy, or world events bring you down. Give it to God to handle. Then, focus on the positive things taking place all around you.

Did you do things differently since COVID-19 impacted your life? Have you been in closer communication with friends and family? Have you found ways to help others in the community who may need assistance meeting basic needs? This is also a good time to reinstitute family dinners, resume work on a hobby, walk outside and enjoy the beauty of nature, catch up on projects around the house, read a book, and indulge yourself with needed rest. Even during the pandemic, there were so many positive things to be thankful for every day.

Thanking God for our many blessings, and putting all our faith and trust in Him, allows us to release any fear and anxiety we may have. As God told the Israelites in Isaiah 41:13: "For *I am the Lord, your God, who takes hold of your right hand and says to you, Do not fear; I will help you.*" Praise the Lord!

23

The Persistent Widow

Jesus' parables can really get us thinking and learning. Today, as we read this parable in Luke, Jesus teaches us a lesson through the example of a persistent widow.

Then Jesus told his disciples a parable to show them that they should always pray and not give up. He said: "In a certain town there was a judge who neither feared God nor cared what people thought. And there was a widow in that town who kept coming to him with the plea, 'Grant me justice against my adversary.' "For some time he refused. But finally he said to himself, 'Even though I don't fear God or care what people think, yet because this widow keeps bothering me, I will see that she gets justice, so that she won't eventually come and attack me!'" And the LORD said, "Listen to what the unjust judge says. And will not God bring about justice for his chosen ones, who cry out to him day and night? Will he keep putting them off? I tell you, he will see that they get justice, and quickly. However, when the Son of Man comes, will he find faith on the earth?"
Luke 18:1-8 (NIV)

Like the widow in the parable, we need to be persistent in our prayer life. In fact, there are scriptures which tell us to pray continually. God will answer our prayers and He will bring justice for His chosen ones who cry out to Him day and night.

When you read the parables in the Bible, do you try to put yourself in the story to understand it better? Can you imagine yourself as the widow? Might you be the judge? Has someone come to you for help, and you ignored their call? Do you care for people, really care for people? Not just in theory, but in practice. The judge sees this woman in need, suffering injustice yet, for a long time, he does nothing. He says nothing. It was not until he felt he could be attacked for his inaction that the judge did anything to provide justice to the widow.

Who could you be helping, serving and defending but you're not? You may say, "Well, haven't done anything bad." Perhaps you did, perhaps you didn't. But if you don't do anything, that IS a bad thing. We can't just have a mindset of compassion, empathy, love, mercy, respect, and generosity. We must have a lifestyle which demonstrates those values.

Are you the widow facing great adversity? She was a powerless and penniless woman facing a powerful and prosperous judge. She wanted justice and she continually pursued it   What do you need to fight for? Don't quit, give up or give in.

If we looked at your schedule, or your budget, does it reveal a heart for people, a fight for justice? Let us NOT be like the judge but let us pray persistently for God to work through us to serve others.

Persistence is positive when the goal is righteous. Persistence in prayer, in faith, and in doing good are all commended because the motivation is right. However, persistence is wrong when the motives are self-serving.

One of the main lessons I have learned over the years is to keep doing good. While doing good sometimes seems fruitless and selfishness seems to be the way to prosper, don't not lose sight of the fact that God does bless those who do good. Be persistent.

24

What's your Status?

Do you have a prestigious job, own a big house, or drive a luxury car? Have you made a name for yourself in your community, your work or at church? We compare ourselves to others in so many aspects of our lives, but it's dangerous when a desire for prestige and power grows stronger than our love and loyalty to God.

Being a religious leader in Jerusalem was quite different than being a pastor today. In Israel, everything in a person's life was centered around its relationship with God. The religious leaders were the best known, most powerful and most respected of all leaders.

However, Jesus said "Everything they do is for show. On their arms they wear extra wide prayer boxes with Scripture verses inside, and they wear robes with extra-long tassels. And they love to sit at the head table at banquets and in the seats of honor in the synagogues. They love to receive respectful greetings as they walk in the marketplaces, and to be called 'Rabbi.'
Matthew 23:5-7 (NLT)

These verses refer to the Pharisees, the religious leaders of the time. The "prayer boxes" were leather boxes containing Scripture verses. The Pharisees wore these as a sign of their love for God and the importance of keeping His commands. It was a good tradition, but it got out of hand. The boxes were made larger than necessary so they could be used as a sign of status...and the "status" of the boxes became more important than the scripture they contained.

Jesus exposed the Pharisees for their hypocritical pursuit of status. Once again, we learn it is not what people see on the outside that is important, but what is in our heart that really matters. Jesus warned His followers not to use the Pharisees as role models for holiness.

The greatest person will be the one who shows His love to the Savior by bending down to serve others. Jesus never asked His followers to do something He had not already done. Jesus, the Son of God had stooped down to serve. Look into Bethlehem's manger and see the baby; stand before Calvary's cross and see the Savior's sacrifice.

Jesus stepped down from His position in heaven to live, suffer, die, and rise again, so all who believe on Him might be saved. Jesus stepped down so you and I might be brought up. Do not live like the Pharisees, focused on outward status, but model your life on Jesus, humbling yourself as you serve God and others.

Matthew 23:11-12 says it well: *The greatest among you must be a servant. But those who exalt themselves will be humbled, and those who humble themselves will be exalted.*

Humility is a greatly under-emphasized quality among humans. Some don't know what it means, don't know how to appreciate it, and aren't all that sure they want to have it.

Culturally we're much more drawn to the energetic, dynamic, charismatic, crowd-drawing leader. That's who gets the headlines and the attention. But if we listen closely and watch carefully, we can see in Jesus someone who is humble, but strong; humble, but charismatic; humble, but crowd drawing; humble, but dynamic.

25

A Solid Foundation

"So why do you keep calling me 'Lord, Lord!' when you don't do what I say? I will show you what it's like when someone comes to me, listens to my teaching, and then follows it. It is like a person building a house who digs deep and lays the foundation on solid rock. When the floodwaters rise and break against that house, it stands firm because it is well built. But anyone who hears and doesn't obey is like a person who builds a house right on the ground, without a foundation. When the floods sweep down against that house, it will collapse into a heap of ruins."
Luke 6:46-49 (NLT)

Why would anyone build a house without a strong foundation? Could it be because they don't want to invest the time and effort to dig down to solid rock? It may be choosing to live on the beach but ignoring the need for recommended hurricane protection/shutters, supports, whatever they do to safeguard homes. I think that shows a lack of preparation for the future...our eternal future. Jesus compared our belief and actions to the foundation of a house.

We can't cut corners when following God. When He gives us direction, which He always does, we must obey. We must put into practice

His teachings. The more committed we are to our relationship with God, and the more we practice His principles, the better prepared we are to handle what life throws our way. Our trust and belief in God are the foundation of our life, demonstrated every day in the things we say and do. If we stand strong on these principles, we can weather the temptations put in front of us without being tempted to give in to them.

If you are a part-time Christian who goes to church regularly, but does not practice Godly principles during the week, you will be held accountable. Jesus exposed those who said religious things but did not have a personal relationship with Him. Many think if they are "a good person" and say religious things, they will have eternal life. However, it is only through faith in Jesus Christ that you will receive eternal life with Him.

Most people do not purposely build their lives on an inferior foundation. They are not intentionally rejecting Jesus' principles; they are just careless in their approach. They don't think about where they're going and the consequences of their actions. When the temptations of life result in poor decisions, everything that has been built up to that time can be swept away and one must start over. It may be time to evaluate where you are in building your foundation.

What are the top 3 values you want to uphold in your own life? Think about how you want others to describe you. What are your current daily habits? Who are the people in your life who make you feel grounded?

Do you need to give yourself up to God and start a new life, a new foundation in Him? Do you need to repair the foundation you have because it has cracks? God knows your heart and the strength of your foundation. Make sure it is solid.

26

Extravagant Love

Then Mary took a twelve-ounce jar of expensive perfume made from essence of nard, and she anointed Jesus' feet with it, wiping his feet with her hair. The house was filled with the fragrance.
John 12:3 (NLT)

Put yourself in Mary's place. It hadn't been that long since she was weeping at Jesus' feet for her dead brother, Lazarus. Jesus raised him from the dead, and now the family was giving a dinner party in Jesus' honor. How could she ever find a way to thank Him?

Martha thanked Jesus through cooking and serving the dinner -- that was her gift. But Mary wanted to do something else. She brought out a treasure -- a flask of pure nard, a fragrant ointment, which was probably the most expensive thing they had in the house. The amount that Mary used was worth a year's wages. She poured it on His feet then wiped them dry with her hair -- unthinkable for a Jewish woman.

Why do this? Anointing was a custom used to honor guests. It was also the way priests were ordained and kings were installed as rulers. The very name "Messiah" (or "Christ") means "the Anointed One." Perhaps all these things were in Mary's heart as she honored Jesus.

When we think about what Jesus has done for us, we find ourselves in Mary's dilemma and wonder how can we adequately thank Him for what He has done? He sought us out, called us to be His own, laid down His life to save us, rose from the dead to give us everlasting life -- how can we ever love Him enough? When words fail us, we look around for some action, some way to say "Thank You. I love You.

Jesus has given us ways to express that love. He has given us Baptism and the Lord's Supper. He has directed us to love and serve our neighbors, even the lowliest, and promised that "..... *whatever you did for one of the least of these brothers of mine, you did for me"* Matthew 25:40 (NIV)

John tells us that the house was filled with the fragrance of the nard. As we seek to love the Lord like Mary loved Him, may the world be filled with the fragrance of our own thank offerings.

We tend to want people to earn love. We want their actions to warrant such extravagant love. It makes us feel like the scales are balanced. There are many reasons as to why. However, I believe God is challenging us to learn to love extravagantly. This is not an overnight process.

We read in the bible about agape love. It is a selfless, unconditional, sacrificial type of love. Agape love is how God loves us and desires to be loved in return. It's an extravagant love. But when we return that love, what does it look like?

It's putting God first and foremost in our lives. It's giving up whatever He asks of us, no matter the cost. It's always obeying Him. It's accepting God's will with joy. It's attempting to love God in the same manner as He loved us—sacrificially, selflessly, unconditionally, and willingly. While it isn't possible to love God to the same degree or extent that He loves us we can at least attempt to love Him in the same way.

27

⊙☙

Jesus Calms a Storm

Have you encountered a time in your life when things seemed to get out of control, and you felt defenseless? Even with God in our lives, we sometimes feel vulnerable. This was the situation with the disciples during Jesus' ministry. Matthew tells us about an incident when a storm came up while they were fishing.

Then Jesus got into the boat and started across the lake with his disciples. Suddenly, a fierce storm struck the lake, with waves breaking into the boat. But Jesus was sleeping. The disciples went and woke him up, shouting, "Lord, save us! We're going to drown!" Jesus responded, "Why are you afraid? You have so little faith!" Then he got up and rebuked the wind and waves, and suddenly there was a great calm. The disciples were amazed. "Who is this man?" they asked. "Even the winds and waves obey him!"
Matthew 8:23-27 (NLT)

In the Sea of Galilee, it was not unusual for storms to appear over the surrounding mountains with little or no warning. To make matters worse, these storms could produce 20-foot waves. The disciples were aware of the dangers of such storms, and they panicked. Even though they had witnessed many miracles performed by Jesus, they were unaware of the magnitude of His power. But God has power over everything, including the storms of nature.

When we understand the power of God over everything, we realize He also has power over the storms in our lives. He can help us with the problems we face. Have you ever cried out to God to save you from a desperate or uncertain situation? There was probably panic in your voice due to the stress. But Jesus would say *"Why are you afraid? You have so little faith!"* Just as we see in the scripture for today, He has it all under control. We are not going to drown. He will get us through the situation safely.

The COVID-19 virus was one of those unexpected storms. How many of us are crying out to God? How many of us heard back "Why are you afraid?" There is a reason we are going through storms like this, and He will use it for our good. I heard about so many families having more time together for meals and activities around the house. There were neighbors helping their fellow neighbors. People realized their helplessness and turning to God for hope. That's what it's all about. We need God. We need to trust in God. God **will** calm the storm.

When we're part of a church family and a storm of life comes along, we have prayer warriors seeking God on our behalf. They're concerned about what we're going through and praying for our wellbeing.

God speaks through other Christians, at times, when we need it most. It's wise to seek counsel from another older Christian who has been there, done that. Their advice is tested and true. They can bring comfort to us and calm our souls.

There are times when we are the ones with the prayers and the needs. Other times, we are the answers to other people's prayers and needs. Sometimes we do not purposely answer prayers, but God works us into the person's life that day, and sometimes just for a minute or two, just to calm their storm. It may be as simple as treating the person behind the counter with respect. Acknowledging the tough job they have and how much they are appreciated. Their storm may be feeling unappreciated.

28

Building Character

Think back through your life and remember the experiences that helped produce your character. Some of them were stressful, I'm sure. Knowing what you do now, how would you get through these same situations if you were facing them today? Would it be easier and less stressful? Too often, we get wrapped up in the moment and think about all the things that can go wrong. Why not just think about all the things that can go right and rejoice in them instead?

The Bible tells us to embrace our struggles and rejoice in them. Paul writes about this in his letter to the believers of Christ in Rome.

We can rejoice, too, when we run into problems and trials, for we know that they are good for us—they help us learn to endure. And endurance develops strength of character in us, and character strengthens our confident expectation of salvation. And this confidence will not disappoint us. For we know how dearly God loves us, because he has given us the Holy Spirit to fill our hearts with his love.

Romans 5:3-5 (NLT)

The tribulations of the early Christians were many and varied. They were hated by the world, tempted by Satan, and corrupted by their own weaknesses. Paul spoke about overcoming these experiences so these young Christians could become the people God wanted them to be. God also has a plan for us and our future.

Did your parents use tough love when raising you? Tough love includes strict disciplinary measures along with enforcing certain constraints on freedoms or privileges, thus requiring children to take responsibility for their actions. My parents used tough love to raise me, and I became a better person because of it. I am grateful for the decisions they made on my behalf.

God uses tough love with His children as well. Because He has control over all things, both good and evil, God could easily give us a life with no problems at all. However, He uses life's difficulties, and Satan's attacks, to build our character. The problems we face develop our patience and endurance, strengthen our character, deepen our trust in God and give us greater confidence in the future. He tells us that we will have tough times in our life, but we can still claim the peace of Christ.

Trials are not the only ingredient to better character. Just as important as the trial itself is the way we respond to them. I think about my approach to customer service. It is easy to give good customer service when things are going smoothly. I see the character of an employee (or business) when things go wrong. How do they handle the situation? How do we handle ourselves when things do not go as expected?

John 16:33 says, *"I have told you all this so that you may have peace in me. Here on earth you will have many trials and sorrows. But take heart, because I have overcome the world."*

Thank God for all the opportunities to build your character through His strength.

29

Just as the Father Does

I was blessed to grow up with a wonderful loving father. I learned many traits that have carried me through life just because I listened to, and watched, him. Among these were honesty, a good work ethic, compassion, humility and faithfulness to God. One way that I can honor my father is to follow in his footsteps, striving to be like him. Not only did Jesus strive to be like His father, God, He *was* God. The Jewish religious leaders did not understand what Jesus was saying and thought it was blasphemy that He claimed to be God.

So Jesus explained, "I tell you the truth, the Son can do nothing by himself. He does only what he sees the Father doing. Whatever the Father does, the Son also does. For the Father loves the Son and shows him everything he is doing. In fact, the Father will show him how to do even greater works than healing this man. Then you will truly be astonished.
John 5:19-20 (NLT)

"The Father and I are one."
John 10:30 (NLT)

I understand it could be hard for people to believe another human saying his father is the almighty, all-powerful God. However, God and Jesus are not only father and son, but they are also the same being. And, because of His unity with his father, Jesus lived as God wanted him to live. When reading this passage, I think about children imitating their parents. Earlier today, I was watching a video of a friend playing his guitar and singing hymns. His young son sat beside him also playing a guitar and singing. This boy wanted to be just like his dad.

Because of our relationship with Jesus, we must honor Him and live as He wants us to live. Do you remember when people wore bracelets with WWJD printed on them? That stood for "What Would Jesus Do?". If we think about this as we're about to make a decision, we might approach things differently. Are we really like Jesus and do we honor Him through our actions?

In today's scripture, Jesus is telling the Jewish leaders that whatever God does, He will also do. Not only that, but God will also show Him how to do even greater things than healing people. We see this when Jesus gave His life to save us from our sins and then conquered death 3 days later when He rose from the dead. All of this was done so that we can have eternal life! Can we live as the Father wants us to live and honor Jesus through our actions?

We honor certain people because they have a perceived value and because of their position. There are biblical instructions for whom we should esteem in this manner. For example, Deuteronomy 5:16 states that we are to honor our parents. Leviticus 19:32 encourages us to honor the elderly. And 1 Peter 2:13 admonishes us to honor those who rule.

One example that Christ gave us is one of service. We honor God when we serve the people around us. We honor Him when we give of ourselves and show others the love that God lavishes on us.

I think about things in my life from the perspective of "what would my father do?" More importantly, however, I think "what would Jesus do?"

30

The First Stone

But early the next morning he was back again at the Temple. A crowd soon gathered, and he sat down and taught them. As he was speaking, the teachers of religious law and the Pharisees brought a woman who had been caught in the act of adultery. They put her in front of the crowd.
"Teacher," they said to Jesus, "this woman was caught in the act of adultery. The law of Moses says to stone her. What do you say?"

They were trying to trap him into saying something they could use against him, but Jesus stooped down and wrote in the dust with his finger. They kept demanding an answer, so he stood up again and said, "All right, but let the one who has never sinned throw the first stone!" Then he stooped down again and wrote in the dust. When the accusers heard this, they slipped away one by one, beginning with the oldest, until only Jesus was left in the middle of the crowd with the woman. Then Jesus stood up again and said to the woman, "Where are your accusers? Didn't even one of them condemn you?"
"No, Lord," she said.
And Jesus said, "Neither do I. Go and sin no more."
   John 8:2-11 (NLT)

How often do we look at another person's sinful behavior and think to ourselves, I would never do that? Our municipal, state and federal laws have different levels of punishment, depending on the crime, yet our society is often quick to prosecute and anxious for punishment. The religious leaders and Pharisees were no different and, according to the laws of God as given to Moses, the punishment for adultery was death by stoning. We read in Leviticus 20:10 (NLT) *"If a man commits adultery with another man's wife, both the man and the woman must be put to death. They are guilty of a capital offense."*

In our first scripture above, the Pharisees were trying to trick Jesus. If He refused to let them stone the woman, He would be violating God's law. If Jesus recommended, they execute her, they would turn Him over to the Romans because it was illegal, according to Roman law, for the Jews to perform their own executions. But Jesus would not fall into their trap. Instead of responding to their question, He bent down to write on the ground. We don't know what Jesus wrote in the dust or if he was just ignoring the accusers.

Jesus' ultimate response was to let them execute the woman caught in adultery, but He stated the one throwing the first stone had to be a person who had never sinned. As all of them had sinned, they gave up and walked away. Like the Pharisees, we too can be quick to judge. How many times have we figuratively "thrown stones" about another person's sins, yet it is God's role, not ours, to judge?

Jesus showed the woman forgiveness and compassion. He let her go away telling her she had not been condemned for her sins by Him or by others. While He did not condone her sin, He did tell her to sin no more. When we confess and repent of our sins, we are forgiven, but that does not give us a free pass to sin as much as we want. With God's help we can accept Christ's forgiveness and change our attitudes and behaviors.

Dear Heavenly Father, thank you for sending your Son, Jesus Christ, to save us from our sins. Please help us to stop judging and "throwing stones." Instead, help us to be more like Jesus, showing forgiveness and compassion to others. Amen.

31

Plant Generously

Remember this—a farmer who plants only a few seeds will get a small crop. But the one who plants generously will get a generous crop. You must each decide in your heart how much to give. And don't give reluctantly or in response to pressure. "For God loves a person who gives cheerfully." And God will generously provide all you need. Then you will always have everything you need and plenty left over to share with others. As the Scriptures say,
"They share freely and give generously to the poor.
Their good deeds will be remembered forever."
For God is the one who provides seed for the farmer and then bread to eat. In the same way, he will provide and increase your resources and then produce a great harvest of generosity in you.
2 Corinthians 9:6-10 (NLT)

I was impressed with the generosity of individuals and businesses during the recent pandemic. Small business owners offered their goods and services for free to health care workers. Individuals gave to local food pantries, animal shelters and other organizations. They did this despite personal financial difficulties or uncertainty.

Some were hesitant to give generously during this time, worried they won't have enough left over to meet their own needs. As Paul assured the Corinthians in the above scripture, God can, and will, meet our needs. As explained in the example of the farmer, those that give generously will receive much more than those who only give a little.

I realize we get frequent calls, emails and Facebook posts asking for countless donations but don't feel pressured to give to everything and everyone. God wants us to give cheerfully, and He will put it on your heart when and where to give. And do not compare your donation to what others are giving. This is not a contest to see who can give the most. We know how God feels about this from the story of the widow's offering in Mark.

Jesus sat down near the collection box in the Temple and watched as the crowds dropped in their money. Many rich people put in large amounts. Then a poor widow came and dropped in two small coins. Jesus called his disciples to him and said, "I tell you the truth, this poor widow has given more than all the others who are making contributions. For they gave a tiny part of their surplus, but she, poor as she is, has given everything she had to live on."
Mark 12:41-44 (NLT)

I am sure you have heard the phrase "You reap what you sow." The point is this: Put down as many seeds as you can, and it will reap what you have put into it. Be faithful to your calling as a farmer. Be faithful to your calling to be Christian. Be faithful to your calling to be parent. Be faithful to your calling to be a friend. If you are lazy in these endeavors, then you will not reap what you want in life. Love demands giving and generosity. Without this, we cannot achieve the purpose of God in our lives. Cynicism or being disgruntled, which leads to stinginess, only gets you isolation. Break free of that bondage.

All the resources we have come from God. They are our "seeds". He wants us to cultivate theses seeds to produce more crops. As you give generously, God will provide more so that your giving can multiply. Use your seeds and plant generously.

32

Get up and Walk

Jesus climbed into a boat and went back across the lake to his own town.
Some people brought to him a paralyzed man on a mat. Seeing their faith,
Jesus said to the paralyzed man, "Be encouraged, my child! Your sins are
forgiven."
But some of the teachers of religious law said to themselves, "That's blasphemy!
Does he think he's God?"
Jesus knew what they were thinking, so he asked them, "Why do you have
such evil thoughts in your hearts? Is it easier to say 'Your sins are forgiven,'
or 'Stand up and walk'? So I will prove to you that the Son of Man has the
authority on earth to forgive sins." Then Jesus turned to the paralyzed man
and said, "Stand up, pick up your mat, and go home!"
And the man jumped up and went home! Fear swept through the crowd as they
saw this happen. And they praised God for giving humans such authority.
  Matthew 9:1-8 (NLT)

  Imagine, for example, going to the doctor for an appendectomy, but
instead of being told your appendix has been removed, the doctor just
says you no longer owe the hospital any money. That's great, but what
does the doctor plan to do about the diseased appendix?

  The situation was much the same for the paralyzed man in our scripture. As he lay on the ground praying for a miracle, Jesus initially told him only that his sins had been forgiven. That was good news, indeed, but not the news the man was expecting! When Jesus then turned around to chat with the Pharisees, I imagine the paralyzed man was quite disappointed that he still could not walk.

The Pharisees, on the other hand, were critical of Jesus, thinking him to be blasphemous when He forgave the man's sins. In their minds, only God had the authority to forgive sins. At that point Jesus turned back to the man, commanding him to stand, pick up his mat, and go home. In doing this, Jesus was showing the Pharisees He IS God, and he DOES have the power to heal both physical and spiritual paralysis. He not only spoke the words of spiritual healing, but He also backed up his words with the physical healing of the man's legs. Jesus gave him a new life!

The paralyzed man did not know Jesus before this incident, but he and his friends had faith in Jesus' healing powers. At the time you and I come to know and believe in Jesus, we too are spiritually healed and cleansed of our sins. When we tell others we believe in God and love him, we need to be sure we back up those words, and demonstrate our love, through the actions of our everyday lives.

Jesus told the man "Stand up, pick up your mat, and go home!" I can only imagine how the man's life was changed and how he shared with others the joy of knowing Christ and the love he experienced. We need to do the same. Jesus Christ has healed us, and He is asking us to get up and walk!

33

Everything is Possible

*Jesus looked at them intently and said, "Humanly speaking, it is impossible.
But with God everything is possible."*
  Matthew 19:26 (NLT)

It's difficult for people to grasp the concept that "everything is possible" because our knowledge of the laws of nature and physics limit the concept of possibility. However, the Bible tells us many times that everything is possible...with God. In this verse, Jesus was explaining to the disciples that rich people can't buy their way into Heaven. With God's help, though, everyone can receive eternal life.

*Then Jesus said to the disciples, "Have faith in God. I tell you the truth, you
can say to this mountain, 'May you be lifted up and thrown into the sea,' and
it will happen. But you must really believe it will happen and have no doubt
in your heart. I tell you, you can pray for anything, and if you believe that
you've received it, it will be yours. But when you are praying, first forgive
anyone you are holding a grudge against, so that your Father in heaven will
forgive your sins, too."*
  Mark 11:22-25 (NLT)

The example of throwing a mountain into the sea was impossible to imagine, but Jesus used it to demonstrate the power of heartfelt prayer for the fruitfulness of God's kingdom. BUT. Don't you just love that word? BUT...there's always a catch.

Certain conditions need to be present for God to answer our prayers. You must have faith in God. You cannot hold a grudge against anyone. The request cannot be selfish in nature, but only for the good of God's Kingdom. Remember to pray for God's will. If our will lines up with God's will, the request will be granted. Jesus prayed this way in the Garden of Gethsemane.

"Father.... everything is possible for you. Please take this cup of suffering away from me. Yet I want your will, not mine."
Mark 14:36 (NLT)

God could have granted Jesus' request to end the suffering, but it was not God's will. How do you pray? Have you ever had prayers you thought were not answered? There is nothing wrong with asking for things that are not humanly possible. We just need to be aware what we are asking for and if it is the will of God to grant our prayer request. Many times, I have prayed for something, and God answered in ways that were completely different than I had anticipated. When I thought back on the experience, I could see He was looking out for me more than I was aware. He took care of my needs instead of my desires, and I was much better off because of His intervention.

God can make anything possible because he has such an expansive and imaginative mind. We cannot even conceive of all He can do. We need to broaden our imagination, our faith in God, our ability to forgive others and our desire for God's will. If we do this, Everything is Possible!

34

Just a Colt

As Jesus and the disciples approached Jerusalem, they came to the town of Bethphage on the Mount of Olives. Jesus sent two of them on ahead. "Go into the village over there," he said. "As soon as you enter it, you will see a donkey tied there, with its colt beside it. Untie them and bring them to me. If anyone asks what you are doing, just say, 'The Lord needs them,' and he will immediately let you take them."

This took place to fulfill the prophecy that said,

"Tell the people of Jerusalem,

'Look, your King is coming to you.

He is humble, riding on a donkey--

riding on a donkey's colt.'"

The two disciples did as Jesus commanded. They brought the donkey and the colt to him and threw their garments over the colt, and he sat on it.

Most of the crowd spread their garments on the road ahead of him, and others cut branches from the trees and spread them on the road. Jesus was in the center of the procession, and the people all around him were shouting,

"Praise God for the Son of David!

Blessings on the one who comes in the name of the Lord!

Praise God in highest heaven!"

The entire city of Jerusalem was in an uproar as he entered. "Who is this?"

they asked.
And the crowds replied, "It's Jesus, the prophet from Nazareth in Galilee."
Matthew 21:1-11 (NLT)

It was just a colt -- a young donkey -- old enough to carry someone safely, but young enough that nobody had trained it yet. It was still with its mother. That young colt was the animal on which Jesus chose to ride into Jerusalem as King and Savior. It was customary for Jewish royalty to ride donkeys or mules, but surely all those animals were well-trained before princes ever sat on them. But riding an unbroken colt is a good way to end up on your backside in the dust!

That's even more likely to happen if the animal you're riding has no proper bridle or saddle, just a cloak or two thrown across its back. With the noise of screaming crowds, the waving of palm branches, and people pressing in close to get a better look, you potentially have a disaster waiting to happen.

But not for Jesus. That unbroken colt carried Him safely and calmly through the crowds, right through the gates of Jerusalem. Jesus' divine power no doubt had something to do with the colt's demeanor, as well as His kindness and forethought in having the colt's older and wiser mother along as well. By evening the two donkeys would have been back home safely, sleeping in peace.

The same could not be said for Jesus Himself. Jesus' own nights of safety could be counted on a single hand -- Sunday, Monday, Tuesday, and Wednesday. Thursday evening, He would eat His last meal with the disciples He loved; a few hours later He would be arrested. There would be no sleep for Him again until after the cross.

Jesus knew this, of course, and He welcomed it. By His suffering and death, He would save all of mankind. His sleep, in death, meant that we would be able to sleep in peace. And His resurrection in joy and power means that we, who belong to Him, can always wake up with trust and hope. Jesus cares for us, even us. For this assurance, there can be no greater proof.

35

The Stones Would Cry Out

What a scene it was with Jesus surrounded by people, all praising God with a loud voice and crying out, "Blessed is the King who comes in the name of the Lord!" What a celebration! Palm branches and cloaks and the sound of rejoicing...with Jesus in the middle of it all.

And some of the Pharisees in the crowd said to him, "Teacher, rebuke your disciples." He answered, "I tell you, if these were silent, the very stones would cry out."
Luke 19:40 (ESV)

Most likely the Pharisees' problem was with the reason for that joy: the crowds were rejoicing because they thought a new king had come to restore their nation to its former glory. Although they were full of excitement and joy, they did not yet realize Jesus was their Messiah. Whatever Jesus' purpose, however, the Pharisees felt threatened and tried to shut down the celebration.

But Jesus wasn't having it and said that if all the people were kept silent the stones along the side of the road would burst into cheers! Even though the crowds of the day didn't recognize Jesus for who he really was, they rejoiced in His presence. It is still natural to rejoice in the Lord and it is right to give Him thanks and praise. As Amos put it, *The Sovereign LORD has spoken— so who can refuse to proclaim his message?* (Amos 3:8b NLT) Joy, speech, and praise flow naturally when God comes to us. Even the stones would cry out.

The Pharisees had stony hearts and sometimes we do as well. We are sometimes insensitive, without compassion or mercy. Jesus came to take our stony hearts and transform them into living, loving hearts that respond to God with joy. Within the week Jesus would do that very thing, laying down His life for our sake and then rising again to live forever. For His sacrifice, the stones themselves, and even us, cry out with joy.

What if you don't feel like praising? Some days life is so hard that praise is the last thing we want to do. We feel like we have little to be thankful for. Although the two are closely intertwined, praise can be distinguished from thanksgiving. Think of praise as saying back to God who He is. "I praise you for your faithfulness. I praise you that you are holy and true. You are my rock and my salvation."

We need to lift our eyes and look at the glory God has set in the heavens. Take a moment to look at the sky above you and consider the greatness of God. Whether you see His glory in a black sky filled with stars or a blue canvas decorated with clouds, it's hard to look at the sky without remembering that God is greater and higher than we are.

If you're struggling to praise today, open your Bible to Psalm 147 and read it out loud. Let it remind you who God really is.

Dear Lord, transform our hearts into loving hearts so we can do your will in our lives. We celebrate Jesus coming to save us and giving us eternal life. We can't thank you enough for this gift! Amen.

36

Clearing the Temple (Again)

Three years before Jesus' death, he traveled to Jerusalem for the celebration of Passover. When He went to the Temple, He did not like what He saw. John 2:13-22 (NLT) tells us what happened.

It was nearly time for the Jewish Passover celebration, so Jesus went to Jerusalem. In the Temple area he saw merchants selling cattle, sheep, and doves for sacrifices; he also saw dealers at tables exchanging foreign money. Jesus made a whip from some ropes and chased them all out of the Temple. He drove out the sheep and cattle, scattered the money changers' coins over the floor, and turned over their tables. Then, going over to the people who sold doves, he told them, "Get these things out of here. Stop turning my Father's house into a marketplace!" Then his disciples remembered this prophecy from the Scriptures: "Passion for God's house will consume me." But the Jewish leaders demanded, "What are you doing? If God gave you authority to do this, show us a miraculous sign to prove it." "All right," Jesus replied. "Destroy this temple, and in three days I will raise it up." "What!" they exclaimed. "It has taken forty-six years to build this Temple, and you can rebuild it in three days?" But when Jesus said "this temple," he meant his own body. After he was raised from the dead, his disciples remembered he had said this, and they believed both the Scriptures and what Jesus had said.

The religious leaders allowed merchants in the courtyard of the temple as a convenience to visitors and to help raise money for temple upkeep. The merchants were dishonest and greedy, and the area was so packed with vendors it was hard for people to worship. Jesus took control of the situation and threw out the merchants and money changers.

Jesus told them to destroy the temple and he would rebuild it in three days. They could not understand that Jesus wasn't talking about the physical building made of stones. He was predicting His own death and resurrection. However, His words planted a seed in the minds of the disciples and the Holy Spirit would prompt them to recall these words when this prediction was fulfilled. The disciples later came to understand Jesus was speaking of His human body as the Temple of God...and that he was, in fact, God! Fast forward three years. When Jesus came to Jerusalem early in the week of His death, He found the same things going on.

Jesus entered the Temple and began to drive out all the people buying and selling animals for sacrifice. He knocked over the tables of the money changers and the chairs of those selling doves. 13 He said to them, "The Scriptures declare, 'My Temple will be called a house of prayer,' but you have turned it into a den of thieves!"
Matthew 21:12-13 (NLT)

Once again, the merchants and money changers were filling the temple courtyard making it difficult for travelers to enter to pray and worship God. In the first cleansing, Jesus was angry about the way business was being conducted, but the second time it was more about the fact they were even doing business at all. Jesus was passionate that his followers should not be hindered when it comes to their relationship with God. We need to honor and worship God without interference or distractions. Knowing this, how are you, as a Christian, respecting and honoring God in what you do? Does your temple need to be cleansed?

37

❦

Judas Agrees to Betray Jesus

Judas was one of the twelve disciples. Why did Jesus pick him? How was it possible for Judas to betray Jesus? Was Judas a bad disciple? Remember, God knows all things...including the future events of our lives...and Judas had a role to place in the prosecution and death of Jesus. Do not forget, that while Judas betrayed Jesus, *all* the disciples eventually abandoned Him. None of them fully understood Jesus or His mission. They were thinking Jesus had come to be their King and ruler of the land. If He was all powerful, why would Jesus be talking about dying?

Then Satan entered into Judas Iscariot, who was one of the twelve disciples, and he went to the leading priests and captains of the Temple guard to discuss the best way to betray Jesus to them. They were delighted, and they promised to give him money. So he agreed and began looking for an opportunity to betray Jesus so they could arrest him when the crowds weren't around.
Luke 22:3-6 (NLT)

Jesus knew all along this would happen...it was part of the plan. Yes, Satan entered Judas, but Judas still had to take responsibility for his part in the betrayal. If we look back at John 17:12 it predicts the future of Judas. Jesus says," *During my time here, I protected them by the power of the name you gave me. I guarded them so that not one was lost, except the one headed for destruction, as the Scriptures foretold.*" And it was Judas that was headed for destruction.

Judas made a commitment to Jesus, and there's no reason to think he was anything but sincere in his faith. Like the rest of the disciples, he left everything to follow our Lord. Judas was actively involved in ministry, and he was given remarkable spiritual gifts. Judas Iscariot was a gospel preacher. He was given the gift of healing, and he exercised authority over demons. Active involvement in ministry is a good and wonderful thing; but it is not a guarantee of spiritual life or health.

In an age when church attendance is down and people are drifting away from the faith they once professed, the story of Judas warns us to guard our hearts, in case we drift away.

Could what happened to Judas also happen to us? Every day, Satan is trying to convince us to do things that are against God's will, but we must resist that temptation. God knows our hearts and will give us direction, but we are still given a choice in how we respond to certain situations in our lives.

We need to search our own hearts and determine how committed are we to God. Are we true disciples and followers, or are we uncommitted pretenders? Do we choose repentance, forgiveness, hope and eternal life, or do we choose despair and death? Because Judas' betrayal sent Jesus to the cross, we are guaranteed the first choice. Will we accept Jesus' gift or, like Judas, will we betray Him?

Even after the betrayal, Judas still had a chance for eternal life. If Judas would have asked for forgiveness, it would have been granted to him. Instead, he chose despair and committed suicide. Let us not follow Judas' example. Jesus has come to take away our despair and gives us life...life eternal!

38

The Passover Lamb

Jesus sent Peter and John ahead to the Upper Room in Jerusalem to prepare for the annual Passover Feast. Passover commemorates the time that God spared the lives of Israel's firstborn sons in Egypt. The book of Exodus tells us the blood of an unblemished, slain lamb was painted on the Israelite's door frames thus causing the plague of the firstborn to pass over their houses. After this plague, Pharaoh freed the Israelites from the bondage of slavery.

During His last meal with the disciples, which has come to be known as The Last Supper, Jesus tried to explain He was about to fulfill the meaning of Passover by giving his body to be broken and his blood to be shed. In this act of sacrifice, Jesus, as the unblemished Lamb of God, would free us from sin and death. He instructed his followers to continually remember his sacrifice by sharing in the elements of bread and wine in the sacrament we have come to know as the Lord's Supper or Communion. One of the places where this event is recorded is in Luke which states:

He took some bread and gave thanks to God for it. Then he broke it in pieces and gave it to the disciples, saying, "This is my body, which is given for you. Do this in remembrance of me."

After supper he took another cup of wine and said, "This cup is the new covenant between God and his people—an agreement confirmed with my blood, which is poured out as a sacrifice for you.

Luke 22:19-20 (NLT)

In offering the bread, Jesus wanted his disciples to remember him, his friendship and his bodily sacrifice for the forgiveness of sin. But the disciples were confused by the comparison of wine to the blood sacrifices with which they were familiar. The disciples had only known of animal blood being offered in sacrifice for sin.

In the Old Testament, God agreed to forgive people's sins if animals were brought to the priests for sacrifice. This ceremonial act had to be repeated regularly. Unlike the blood of animals, however, Jesus' blood would remove the sins of all who believed in Him. Jesus' sacrifice would never have to be repeated.

In modern times. we are often repulsed by the very idea of killing an animal. The Israelites were herdsmen. Our ancestors, and some of our relatives, were (are) farmers. But we city folk don't routinely butcher animals, drain out their blood, and cut them up. The closest we come is cold meat in a Styrofoam tray or butcher's wrap from the grocery store. We eat meat, for the most part, but we are insulated from the killing that is required.

Nevertheless, taking of any life should affect us as it affected the Israelites. The Israelites were very aware that blood required taking of life. And taking life, even to eat, is never a trivial thing. God tells Moses:

"For the life of a creature is in the blood, and I have given it to you to make atonement for yourselves on the altar; it is the blood that makes atonement for one's life."

Leviticus 17:11 (NIV)

Jesus dying on the cross for us is not a trivial thing. Jesus is the Lamb of God who takes away the sins of the world! Let us never forget this as we praise God for His love every day of our lives. For through the sacrifice of this Passover Lamb, we will have eternal life! Hallelujah!!!

39

Your Will, Not Mine

"Father, if you are willing, please take this cup of suffering away from me. Yet I want your will to be done, not mine." Then an angel from heaven appeared and strengthened him. He prayed more fervently, and he was in such agony of spirit that his sweat fell to the ground like great drops of blood.
Luke 22:42-44 (NLT)

Even while praying in the Garden of Gethsemane, Jesus knew He was about to be betrayed, denied, and rejected by His disciples and followers. Trials, torture and death by crucifixion were in His immediate future. He expressed His concerns to God, but He still put the father's will before His own. The verse says, *"Then an angel from heaven appeared and strengthened him"* so he might be able to go forward with His mission.

Jesus' example ought to be a comfort to us. Prayer was a way of life for Jesus, even when his human desires ran contrary to God's. We can pour out our honest desires to God, even when we know they conflict with His, even when we wish with all our body and soul that God's will could be done in some other way.

In the darkest hours of Jesus' suffering, as He hung on the cross, Jesus cried out the opening words of Psalm 22, *"My God, my God, why have you forsaken me?"* Although much has been suggested regarding the meaning of this phrase, we know with certainty it shows the agony Christ felt as he experienced separation from God. Here we see the Father turn away from the Son as Jesus bore the full weight of all our sins, without exception.

Billy Graham said it this way "He was without sin, for He was God in human flesh. But as He died all our sins were placed on Him, and He became the final and complete sacrifice for our sins. And in that moment, He was banished from the presence of God, for sin cannot exist in God's presence." However, despite the enormous degree of pain and suffering, both physical and spiritual, Jesus did not question God's will.

Then Jesus, calling out with a loud voice, said, "Father, into your hands I commit my spirit!" And having said this he breathed his last.
Luke 23:46 (ESV)

Jesus was truly committed to His mission. He was doing God's will, despite the suffering he would endure, to save us from our sins so we might never experience eternal separation from God. Imagine such a powerful love! John 3:16 tells us "For God so loved the world that he gave his one and only Son, that whoever believes in Him shall not perish but have eternal life." We are not worthy of this kind of love, but He loves us anyway. Rejoice in the Lord, for He has given up ALL for us!

Dear Heavenly Father, thank you that we, like Jesus, can bring all our fears and concerns to you. And thank you for giving us the strength to endure whatever pains and struggles we may suffer, especially during the uncertainties of the current worldwide pandemic. Provide us the wisdom to understand your will and the strength to commit to it as Jesus did. We cannot thank you enough for all the love you show us. Guide us to share this love with others. In Jesus' name we pray. Amen.

40

He is not Here. He is Risen!

Early on Sunday morning, as the new day was dawning, Mary Magdalene and the other Mary went out to visit the tomb. Suddenly there was a great earthquake! For an angel of the Lord came down from heaven, rolled aside the stone, and sat on it. His face shone like lightning, and his clothing was as white as snow. The guards shook with fear when they saw him, and they fell into a dead faint.

Then the angel spoke to the women. "Don't be afraid!" he said. "I know you are looking for Jesus, who was crucified. He isn't here! He is risen from the dead, just as he said would happen. Come, see where his body was lying. And now, go quickly and tell his disciples that he has risen from the dead, and he is going ahead of you to Galilee. You will see him there. Remember what I have told you."
Matthew 28:1-7 (NLT)

Imagine the astonishment and apprehension the women felt when they saw the angel and heard the news he shared! They had come to put burial spices on Jesus' body, but the tomb was empty. The angel told them Jesus was not there, but they should not be afraid. He had been raised from the dead just as He promised. Then the angel sent them off to share the good news with the disciples.

Even though Jesus had prophesied about His death and resurrection on numerous occasions, no one really expected to see an empty tomb or find Him alive. It took proof for them to truly believe, and proof they had when Jesus soon appeared before the disciples and more than 500 others. The resurrection became the foundation of our faith and removed any doubt Jesus was the Messiah!

And if Christ has not been raised, then your faith is useless, and you are still under condemnation for your sins.
  1 Corinthians 15:17 (NLT)

He was handed over to die because of our sins, and he was raised from the dead to make us right with God.
  Romans 4:25 (NLT)

History shows us we are not without dark times. We can identify periods when evil and darkness seemed to be in control. We can look back on our own lives and recall times of grief, hurt, loneliness, or despair. Or maybe those times are happening right now, and life seems empty of meaning or purpose.

Jesus knows what that's like—and even more. On the cross he suffered the agony of complete separation from God (descending into hell) so that we wouldn't have to—and his body was placed in a tomb till he rose to life again on the third day.

As we celebrate Easter, let us remember Jesus was our sacrificial Lamb, paying the sin debt for our salvation. He erased our sins by His death on the cross and resurrection three days later. When we accept Jesus Christ as our Savior, He forgives our sins and makes us right with God. What a blessing! Now it is our time, like Mary Magdalene and the disciples, to share the Good News. Let's not keep it a secret.

Jesus is not in the tomb—**He Is Risen! He is Risen Indeed!**

Scripture References

Notes

Bible verses were used from the following sources.

English Standard Version (ESV)
The Holy Bible, English Standard Version. ESV® Text Edition: 2016.
Copyright © 2001 by Crossway Bibles, a publishing ministry of Good News Publishers.

New English Translation (NET)
NET Bible® copyright ©1996-2017 by Biblical Studies Press, L.L.C.
http://netbible.com All rights reserved.

New International Version (NIV)
Holy Bible, New International Version®, NIV® Copyright ©1973, 1978, 1984, 2011 by Biblica, Inc.®

New Living Translation (NLT)
Holy Bible, New Living Translation, copyright © 1996, 2004, 2015 by Tyndale House Foundation.

New Life Version (NLV)
Copyright © 1969, 2003 by Barbour Publishing, Inc.

Thomas Mayberry's passion is teaching people how to take their faith in God and apply it in their personal and professional roles. He has published books on leadership, stress management, and goal setting. Learn more about building a relationship with God through his website https:/thomasamayberry.com

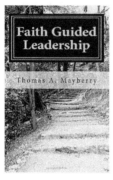

What defines your leadership style? Are you reaching your potential as a leader? How would your leadership style change if you had God in the center of your life? If you let Him guide you towards being a more effective leader, how much of a difference would it make?

The qualities of a strong leader are given to us in the Bible. God has shown us the path to fulfilling our potential. Do we ignore Him and fall prey to the ways of the world, or do we follow His teachings and positively influence all of the people that we associate with? The choice is yours.

This book is written from the perspective of a manager who was trying to fit into corporate America. Tom took on the same traits as the people that he reported to. He felt that the way to succeed was to learn from those that had succeeded before him. It took 20 years and almost two marriages for him to learn where to put his priorities. Once he refocused his life to God, it has shown through in his style of leadership. Today, he stays true to his faith in God and does not worry about what others think is the only way to lead a team. He knows the one true way.

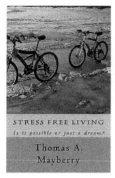

I have been blessed with the ability to stay calm and relaxed in most areas of my life. I have also seen the other end of the spectrum of stress in my life. Writing this book has opened my eyes to the area of my life that I was not completely honest with myself as to my stress level. I am going to share some of the stress reducing techniques with you throughout this book. If it came down to just using techniques, though, we would all be living stress free. You need to approach stress management with the right attitude. I apply a Christian approach, as I do in most areas of my life. This has made a huge impact in my life. When I bottomed out in stress several years ago, it was my Christian fellowship that pulled me out of it. I have grown closer in my walk with God and see the difference it has made in my ability to handle stress.

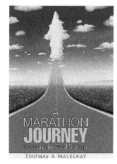

A Marathon Journey is an inspirational look at how you can achieve your goals no matter how daunting they may seem. This is told through the point of view of a man in his fifties that pursued running as a way to lose weight. The author had never run more than a mile at a time in his life and within eighteen months, was able to run three half marathons and a full marathon. Thomas breaks down goal setting into manageable steps to enable you to achieve even your most elusive goals.

Lightning Source UK Ltd.
Milton Keynes UK
UKHW041942180123
415593UK00002B/8